For Grandpa Fred
—H.M.Z.

Text copyright © 2005, 2023 by Harriet Ziefert
Illustrations copyright © 2005, 2023 by Amanda Haley
All rights reserved / CIP Data is available.
Published in the United States by
🍎 Blue Apple Books
South Orange, New Jersey
www.blueapplebooks.com

40 USES
for a
GRANDPA

Harriet Ziefert
drawings by Amanda Haley

BLUE APPLE BOOKS

1. play date

2. veterinarian

3. cash machine

4. taxi

5. e-pal

6. farmer

7. nurse

8. judge

9. mediator

10. coach

11. referee

12. butler

13. pet minder

14. oarsman

15.
dance partner

16. teacher

17. hand warmer

18. chef

19. entertainment center

20. cheerleader

21. flight attendant

22. handyman

23. bug catcher

24. architect

25. storyteller

26. ticket holder

27. shelf

28. photo album

29. partner

30. adding machine

31. basketball hoop

32. dictionary

33. tailor

34. baker

35. opponent

36.
valentine

37. assistant

38. toy maker

39. worm handler

40. Friend

HARRIET ZIEFERT is the grandmother of Will, Nate, Sylvie, Charlie and Lucy. She is the well-known author of more than two hundred books for children.

AMANDA HALEY collects antique toys, which often appear in her artwork. A graduate of The School of the Art Institute of Chicago, she now lives in Ohio with her husband, Brian, and their golden retriever, Sally.